Pearson Scott Foresman Reading Street
Practice Stations
Management Handbook

Glenview, Illinois
Boston, Massachusetts
Chandler, Arizona
Upper Saddle River, New Jersey

ISBN-13: 978-0-328-38465-5
ISBN-10:   0-328-38465-8

2 3 4 5 6 7 8 9 10   12 11 10 09
CC1

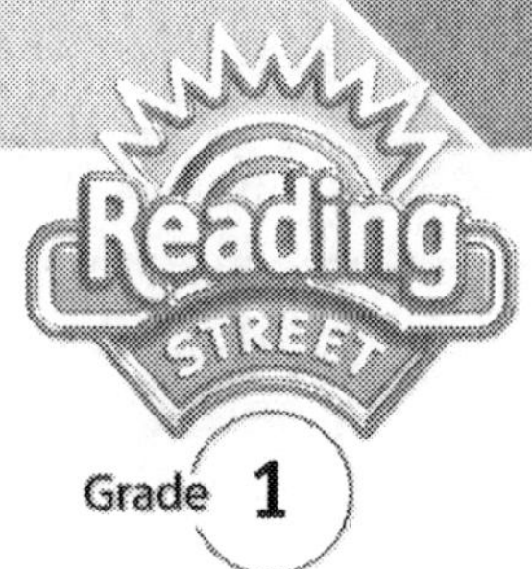

Table of Contents

Welcome to Practice Station Time!

The Pearson Scott Foresman Reading Street Practice Stations Kit helps simplify the task of managing centers by providing ideas for setting up classroom stations, weekly activities for each station, and suggested student routines for each station.

Pearson Scott Foresman Reading Street Practice Stations Kit Components

Practice Station Management Poster

One of the keys to making Practice Station time productive is for children to know at which station they should be working each day. With this write-on/wipe-off poster, you can label the stations for the week and list children's names for each station.

Practice Station Icons

Use Practice Station Icons to tell children which stations they can visit on any particular day or week. You can apply these icons to the Practice Stations Management Poster interchangeably.

Practice Station Flip Charts

The Practice Station Flip Charts are tabletop-sized flip charts that complement the Practice Station activities in the Teacher's Edition. Each flip-chart page lists materials needed for and describes, in child-friendly language, the weekly activity for that station. There are four flip charts, one each for the Word Work, the Writing, the Science/History-Social Science, and the Technology Practice Stations. The activities provide opportunities for children to practice skills and to expand knowledge of the weekly concept across a variety of content areas.

Setting Up the Practice Stations

The classroom environment is an important factor in children's learning. Create separate spaces for the different types of instruction and activities that take place.

How can I set up the Practice Station?

The thought of setting up stations in your classroom can be a bit daunting. This is especially true if you have a small classroom. Making room for stations can be accomplished if you start by thinking of them as extensions of your lessons.

- A Practice Station does not need to be large. A comfortable pillow in a cozy corner makes a great Reading Practice Station.

- With young children, pick a location for a station and maintain that location throughout the year.

- Set up your Practice Stations so that children will not distract those working independently or with you in a small group.

Productive Practice Station Time

By taking time in the beginning to "teach" the Practice Station, your Practice Stations will enhance the learning in your room! Have fun with the stations; they are a powerful piece of your curriculum.

- Tell children what types of materials are in each Practice Station.

- Use the Management Lessons to introduce each station and model how to use the materials.

- Tell them what they will practice in each station. Explain the activity options provided in each station if they finish the assigned activity early.

- Have children role play for the class appropriate behavior and possible situations they may encounter in the center.

- Explain how "My Work Plan" can help them keep track of the tasks they have completed.

- With young children it is often best to gradually add stations. Too much too soon is overwhelming!

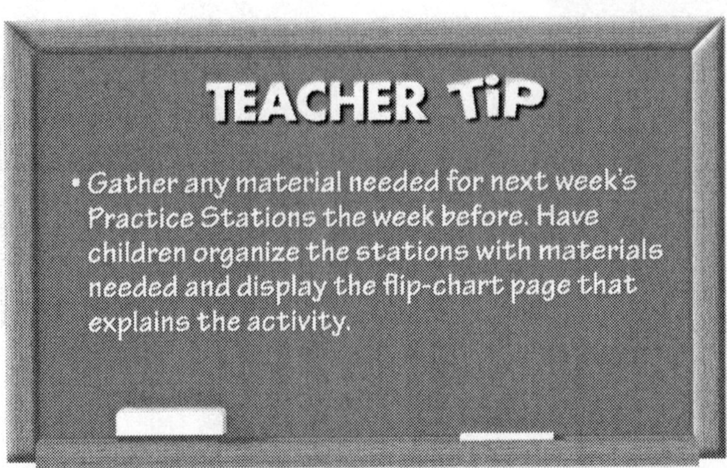

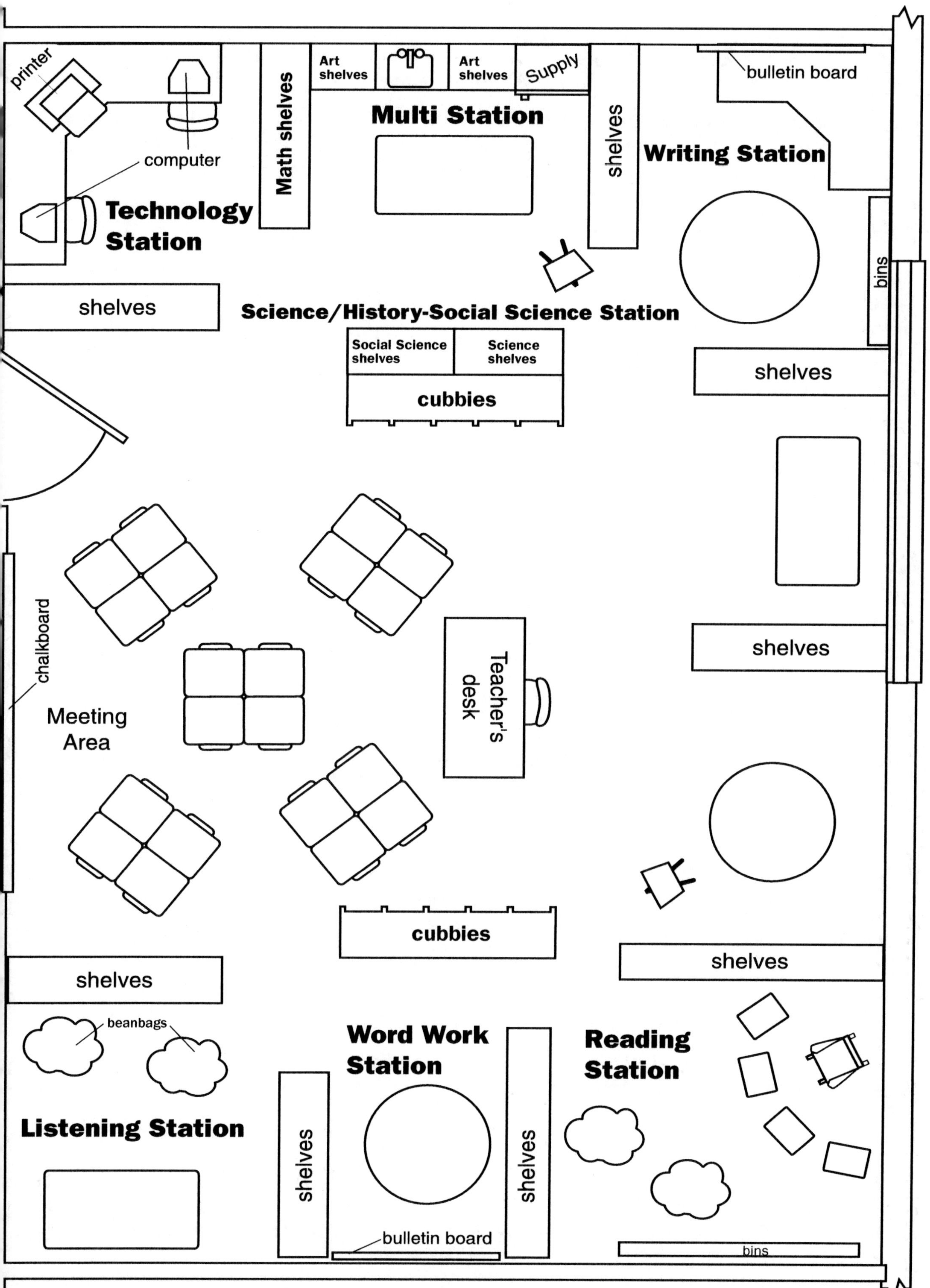

printer
computer
Technology Station
shelves
Math shelves
Art shelves
Art shelves
Supply
Multi Station
shelves
bulletin board
Writing Station
bins
Science/History-Social Science Station
Social Science shelves
Science shelves
cubbies
shelves
shelves
chalkboard
Meeting Area
Teacher's desk
shelves
cubbies
shelves
shelves
beanbags
Listening Station
Word Work Station
Reading Station
shelves
bulletin board
shelves
bins

Listening Practice Station

At the Listening Practice Station, children can listen to previously recorded stories, songs, plays, and rhymes. The CDs at the station serve as models of fluency, intonation, and pronunciation, and they can help reinforce decoding and oral-reading strategies.

Setting Up the Practice Station

The Listening Practice Station can be set up on a table or on the floor in a corner of the classroom.

- Locate the station near an electrical outlet to plug in the compact disc player.

- Have headsets so that children listening to the AudioText CD can "tune out" classroom distractions.

Materials

- CDs that build background for reading selections

- Copies of reading selections

- Commercially made recordings on audio tape or CD

- Thematic and content-area audio tapes or CDs (These can be made by teachers, children, and/or parents.)

Listening Practice Station

Management Lesson   Using Equipment

Materials   chart paper, markers, CD player, headphones, Audio-Text CD, Student Edition

Introduce   Today we're going to practice using equipment in the Listening Station. Do you ever listen to CDs? What do you listen to? Here we will listen to the story in your book. Why is it a good idea to listen to a story as we read it? That's right, it helps us understand what we're reading. It also helps us with words we might have trouble with.

Model   On a piece of chart paper, write *CD Player Controls.* Below the heading, draw pictures of the symbols on the CD player control buttons: Open/Close, Play, Stop, Pause, Forward, and Back. Ask the children to suggest what each symbol means. Write the meanings next to the symbols. Supply any answers the children don't know.

Model putting on the headphones, making sure the children understand they should cover their ears completely. Then model inserting an AudioText CD and using the controls. Put the accompanying book in front of you. This is how I read the story as I listen to the AudioText.

Guide practice   Now it's your turn. Have the group imitate your actions as you again model using the CD player and putting on the headphones.

On their own   Let's all practice using the equipment. Have the children work independently. Circulate among the group, making sure that they are following along in their books. Give corrective feedback as necessary.

MANAGEMENT TIP

If children lose their place in their book as they read, have them track the print. Model and provide corrective feedback as necessary.

Reading Practice Station

At the Reading Practice Station, children can read by themselves or with a partner. They can make connections across texts, explore personal interests, or find out more about topics, authors, and genres.

Setting Up the Practice Station

Find a comfortable space for this station away from the main activity of the classroom.

- Include a table and chairs as well as rocking chairs, carpet squares, or beanbags.

- Use shelves, wire rack bins, or plastic tote trays to create an organized classroom library.

- Gradually add and take away books to avoid having too many books, which can overwhelm children.

- Group books by theme, topic, genre, reading level, or author.

Materials

- Content Readers

- Books by topics and themes

- Books by favorite authors

- Class-made books

- Copies of My Reading Log (p. 70)

Reading Practice Station

Management Lesson 1   Independent Reading

Materials   chart paper, markers, self-selected books

Introduce   Today we're going to practice how to read independently. Why is it important for us to spend time reading on our own? That's right, reading independently is fun. We get to choose our own books and learn about things we find interesting. Independent reading also helps us become better readers. It allows us to practice the skills and strategies we learn in class.

Model   **Using a self-selected book, model reading independently.** When I read independently, I sit where my classmates won't disturb me. I read silently or in a low voice so that I don't disturb others. I quickly find my place in my book, and I read until time is up. Watch as I read. **Model reading independently.**

Write *Rules for Independent Reading* at the top of a piece of chart paper. What did you notice about my independent reading? **As children respond, restate their observations as rules and record the rules on the chart.**

Guide practice   Now it's your turn. **Have the group imitate your actions as you again model appropriate reading behaviors.** What did you notice about our reading? This is the way I want you to read independently.

On their own   Let's all practice independent reading. When I call your name, take your book and find a spot where you can read without being disturbed. Make sure you are using the reading behaviors we listed on our chart. We will read for three minutes. I will let you know when time is up. **Gradually dismiss individuals.** **As children read, circulate around the room providing feedback.**

MANAGEMENT TIP

Start off slowly, gradually increasing the amount of time children spend reading independently. Model and provide corrective feedback as necessary.

Reading Practice Station

Management Lesson 2   Choosing Appropriate Books

Materials   classroom books and other reading materials

Introduce   Why do we read? That's right, we read for fun or to learn about interesting things. Sometimes we read because we like the illustrations in a book. Today we're going to practice choosing books. In the classroom, what can we choose from? **As children answer, hold up examples of the materials they mention. But** how do we choose what we want to read at a particular time?

Model   **Model choosing a book.** Before I pick something to read, I think about *why* I'm going to read. Do I want to find out more about something I'm learning at school? Do I want to read for fun? Do I want to read something I've read before? Let's say we talked about pets in class, and I wanted to learn more about them. I'll look for something new to read about pets. **Model selecting a book or story about a pet.** Now I carefully skim through the book to see how many words are on a page and if the words are too hard or too easy. This one looks just right for me!

Guide practice   Now it's your turn. **Give children a topic and have the group choose a book to read. Guide their deliberation, asking questions about their purpose for reading. Then skim through the book with them.** Are the words on the page too hard, too easy, or just right? **Make sure children know what materials are available and where to find them.**

On their own   Let's all practice choosing books. **Depending on the accessibility of reading materials, call on children singly or in small groups to make their selections. Model and provide feedback as necessary.**

MANAGEMENT TIP

Tell children that sometimes we read a book because we like the author or illustrator. Model how to find more books by the same author or illustrator.

12

Reading Practice Station

Management Lesson 3 Using a Reading Log

Materials chart; paper; markers; copies of My Reading Log, p. 70; pencils

Introduce Today we are going to practice using a reading log. Do you know what a reading log is? That's right, a reading log is a record of books we've read. Why is it important to keep a record of what we've read? Yes, when we keep a reading log we always know which books we've read and when we read them. A reading log can show us what books we find interesting. It can also show us how our reading has improved throughout the year.

Model Watch as I write information in this log. **Model filling in a reading log by making a quick replica of My Reading Log, p. 70, on chart paper. I** always write my name on my reading log. Then I write today's date. Next, I think about what I read today. **Continue filling in the log, using class texts and other stories and books children might be familiar with. As you mention them, write the titles and authors on the chart paper. Point out that you are including things you've read outside of class.** The last column is where I write my opinion of, or what I thought about, the story or book.

My Reading Log

Date	What is the title?	Who is the author?	What did you think of it?
Nov. 2, 2010	*Snap!*	Jacqui Briggs	I liked it.

Guide practice Next, let's make a log for the whole class. **Flip to the next blank page on the chart, and write** *Our Reading Log.* **Have the group suggest titles they've all read, listing the titles as the children mention and agree on them. If children forget or do not know the author of a book, show them where to find this information.**

On their own Now it's your turn. **Distribute copies of My Reading Log and have children create their own reading logs. As they write, move among them, providing feedback as necessary.**

MANAGEMENT 

If children would like to add more information to their reading logs, suggest they write about their favorite part of the book, how many pages they read, or what the genre is. Model and give corrective feedback as necessary.

# Word Work Practice Station

For many teachers, setting up the Word Work Practice Station presents the biggest challenge because of the wide range of abilities among children. You need to have the greatest variety of materials and options to meet the needs of all children.

The Word Work Practice Station is the place where children will need the most support.

Setting Up the Practice Station

The Word Work Practice Station is the place where children can demonstrate what they have learned in phonemic awareness and phonics. Children can build words with letter tiles and then write the words on a word list or sort pictures by initial, medial, or final sounds.

As you review the work children do in the Word Work Practice Station, look to see whether they are demonstrating an understanding of the phonemic awareness and phonics skills you have taught.

- Are they applying the target skill?
- Are they also applying previously learned skills to their work?

Materials

- Letter Tiles
- Magnetic Letters and Boards
- Picture Cards
- Sound Spelling Charts
- Finger Tracing Cards
- Paper
- Pencils
- Crayons
- Decodable Readers
- Write-On/Wipe-Off Boards
- Dictionaries and Pictionaries

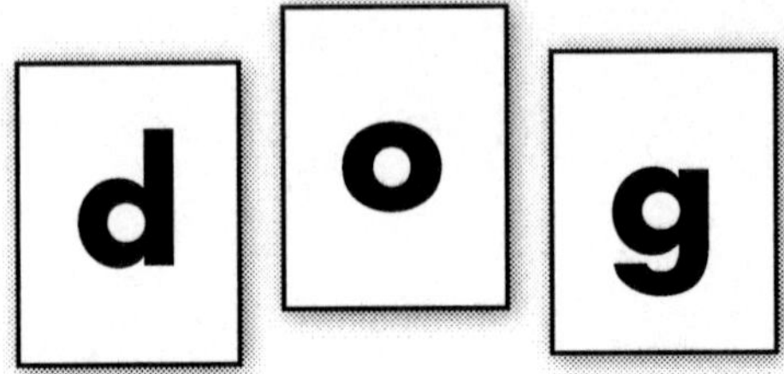

Word Work Practice Station

Management Lesson 1 Working with a Partner

Materials chart paper, markers, word cards

Introduce Today we're going to practice working with a partner. Why is it important for us to work with someone else? That's right, when we work together, we help each other understand things and learn how to share ideas. When we work with a partner, it is important to take turns, to talk quietly, and to be polite.

Model Ask a child to help you model working with a partner. First, model working side-by-side. Sit next to the child and place the writing materials in front of both of you on the table. When you need to read or work together, sit next to one another, or side-by-side, so that both of you can see your work. Next, move to sit opposite the child, placing the materials between you. When you are going to play a game, you need to sit face-to-face, with the game between you.

Model speaking quietly, being polite, making suggestions, and problem-solving as you sort words.

Write *Rules for Partner Work* at the top of a piece of chart paper. As I worked with my partner, how did I sit? As children respond, restate their observations as rules and record the rules on the chart.

Rules for Partner Work

- Sit side-by-side to work together.
- Sit face-to-face to play a game.
- Take turns.
- Talk quietly.
- Be polite.

Guide practice Now it's your turn. Assign the children partners, and assign each partnership a Partner A and a Partner B. Tell them to begin by sitting side-by-side. Have the group practice appropriate pair-work behaviors as they sort words. Tell them that Partner A should begin and that Partner B should listen while Partner A talks. Then have them sit face-to-face and play a word-reading game. Tell them that now it is Partner B's turn, so Partner A should not interrupt. Provide corrective feedback as necessary.

On their own Let's all practice working with a partner. Have each pair of children sort words. As they work, circulate around the room and provide feedback as necessary.

MANAGEMENT TIP

Tell children it's acceptable for partners to disagree as they work, but that they should work together quietly and politely to come up with a solution to a problem. Model and provide corrective feedback as necessary.

# Word Work Practice Station

Management Lesson 2 Sorting Words

Materials chart paper, markers, word cards

Introduce Today we are going to practice sorting words. What does it mean to sort something? Yes, it means to put things that are alike in separate groups. What kinds of things have you sorted? That's right, you sort your toys. You might put all your stuffed animals in one place, all your wooden toys in another place, and all your action figures in still another place. When we sort words, we separate them into groups with the same sound.

Model Using cards you've prepared in advance, model how to sort words. Explain that for word-sorting tasks, the children may be given lists of words, or they may be given cards with words already printed on them. Show them four cards printed with the following words: *hop, mad, pat, stop.* I have four cards with words on them. Some have a short *o* sound in the middle and some have a short *a* sound. When I read these words aloud, I can hear the differences in how they sound. **Model sorting the cards, reading the words aloud as you do so.**

Guide practice Now it's your turn. **Take the next set of cards. They should be printed with these words:** *kid, cap, snap, mud.* Here we need to pay attention to the last sound in each word. If the word ends in /d/ spelled *d*, we'll put it in one pile. If it ends in /p/ spelled *p*, we'll put it in another pile. **Have the children read each word and tell you which pile to put it in. Correct and provide feedback as necessary.**

On their own Let's all practice sorting words. **Distribute sets of words cards to the children, and have them sort them according to the rules you've determined for the sorting activity. Circulate around the room, providing corrective feedback.**

MANAGEMENT TIP

When children sort words, make sure they understand the rules by which they're sorting. As they work, model and provide corrective feedback as necessary.

Word Work Practice Station

Management Lesson 3   Building Words

Materials   letter tiles

Introduce   Today we are going to practice building words. What does it mean to build something? That's right, to build something means to put something together. We build towers by putting blocks together. Workers build bridges by putting steel parts together. When we build words, we put letters together. We blend the letters to make a word.

Model   Now we are going to build words with the short *a* sound. **Write *rat* on the board and blend it.** Watch me change /r/ in *rat* to /s/. **Model blending the new word *sat*.** Now watch me change /s/ in *sat* to /p/. **Model blending the new word *pat*.**

Guide practice   Now it's your turn. **Give each child letter tiles *a, f, m, n, t*. Write *fan* and have the group blend it with you. Have children spell *fan* with letter tiles.** Now change /f/ in *fan* to /t/. **Let's say the new word together. Continue the activity with *m*. Monitor children's work.**

On their own   Let's all practice building words. **Have each child work with a partner. Distribute letter tiles to each pair of children, start them off with a three-letter short *a* word, and then have them build more words by replacing initial or final letters. As they build words, circulate around the room, providing corrective feedback and modeling as necessary.**

MANAGEMENT TIP

If possible, have children write a list of the words they are building. Model and provide corrective feedback as necessary.

Writing Practice Station

The Writing Practice Station is another place where you need to address a wide range of abilities. Children need to begin at their own level. The more you provide in the station, the more successful it will be for all. As you review the work children do in the Writing Practice Station, look to see whether they are applying the phonics skill you have introduced. Writing is an excellent way to assess phonetic development.

Setting Up the Practice Station

The Writing Practice Station may need more space than other stations.

- Designate a table for children who are working on prewriting and drafting activities and another for revising, editing, and publishing.

- Set up computers for word processing on another table or on a group of desks.

- Write the Amazing Words for the week on index cards and place them in the center. Encourage children to write using the Amazing Words.

- Write children's names on large cards. You may wish to attach their picture. Encourage children to write about their friends.

- Place envelopes and a class mailbox in the center; children can write and "mail" letters.

Materials

- Paper in different sizes, shapes, colors, and textures

- Pencils, markers, crayons, scissors, glue, glitter, yarn, hole punch

- Magazines, catalogs, or other sources of pictures that can be cut up

- Word banks, dictionaries, writer's handbooks

- Prewriting graphic organizers and revising and editing checklists

Writing Practice Station

Management Lesson 1 Working in the Writing Station

Materials chart paper, markers, writing materials

Introduce Today we're going to talk about writing. What sorts of things do we write? That's right, sometimes we write lists, sometime we write sentences, sometimes we write e-mails, and sometimes we write stories. Why is it important to write things? Yes, we write to remind ourselves of things, to do homework, and to communicate with people. Sometimes we even write for fun! In the Writing Station, there are small assignments to help us practice writing.

Model Here's an example of something you might find in the Writing Station. **On the board, write this sentence frame:** *At the beach, I like to _____.* I'm going to copy the sentence frame on my own paper and then fill in the blank. **Model copying the sentence and filling in the blank, keeping your eyes on your paper. Then show the paper to the class.** When I am at the beach, I like to go in the water and swim. So I wrote the sentence, filling in the blank with the word *swim.*

Write *Rules for Writing* at the top of a piece of chart paper. What did you notice about what I did while I was writing? **As children respond, restate their observations as rules and record the rules on the chart.**

Guide practice Now it's your turn. **Have the children suggest other ways of completing the sentence frame and write sentences on the chart that incorporate their suggestions. Tell them to copy one of the completed sentences on their own papers.**

On their own Let's all practice writing. **Write the following sentence frame on the board:** *My favorite color is _____.* Let's all practice writing. **Have the children write the sentence frame on their own papers and fill in the blank appropriately. As they work, circulate around the room providing feedback.**

MANAGEMENT TIP

Be sure children know where materials in the Writing Station are kept and when to use each one. Model and provide corrective feedback as necessary.

Writing Practice Station

Management Lesson 2 Following Directions

Materials chart paper with pre-written directions, writing materials, copies of a simple Writing Station activity

Introduce Today we're going to practice following directions. Why is it important to follow directions? That's right, we follow directions to stay safe, to be healthy, and to do well in school. Sometimes we listen to directions and follow them and sometimes we read directions and follow them. Often the directions we follow in school are written. We have to read them in order to know what to do.

Model Watch as I follow written directions. **Show children these written directions:**

1. **Write your name on your paper.**
2. **Write a word that begins with** *m.*
3. **Circle the** *m.*

Writing on the board and reading each one aloud as you write, follow these directions. It is very important that we read every step in a list of directions and that we understand exactly what we are supposed to do.

Guide practice Now it's your turn. **Lead the group in reading the directions. Have them follow each step as they read. What might happen if you didn't read the first step?** That's right, if you didn't write your name on your paper, I wouldn't know who wrote it.

On their own Let's all practice following directions. **Give children a copy of a simple Writing Station activity. Tell them to read the directions step by step and follow them. Encourage children to ask questions if they aren't sure what to do. Circulate around the room, providing feedback.**

MANAGEMENT 

After children follow directions, have them reread each step to make sure they followed the directions completely. Model and give corrective feedback as necessary.

Science Practice Station

The Science Practice Station is a wonderful place to discover! The *Pearson Scott Foresman Reading Street Practice Stations* pages in the Teacher's Edition give you detailed information to make your Science Practice Station specific to your weekly concept.

Setting Up the Practice Station

- Create a "Discovery Journal" for children to document observations in the Science Station over time.

- During each science topic, children can complete simple experiments in the center or extensions of the lesson, such as documenting the growth of seeds.

- Post Amazing Words related to science in the Science Station for children to use in their writing.

Materials

- Measuring cups

- Sand or rice

- Pictures of animals

History-Social Science Practice Station

The History-Social Science Practice Station is a place where children can explore their school, town, state, the United States, and the world. The *Pearson Scott Foresman Reading Street Practice Stations* pages in the Teacher's Edition give you detailed information to make your History-Social Science station specific to your weekly concept.

Setting Up the Practice Station

- Create an "Exploration Journal" for each child.

- Post Amazing Words related to social science in the History-Social Science Station for children to use in their writing.

- If the content of your main selection is social science, place a copy of the Student Edition in the station.

- Place books related to the topic you are studying in the station to bring additional literacy activities to the social science content.

Materials

- Maps

- Globes

- Geography puzzles

Science/Social Science Station

Management Lesson 1 Locating Information

Materials chart paper, markers, grade-level science and social science books

Introduce Today we're going to practice how to find information. What is information? That's right, information is facts about something or someone. Some information about bees is that they make honey. Some information about George Washington is that he was the first President of the United States. We learn new information every day. But how do we find it on our own?

Model **Using a book related to the weekly concept, model looking through the book. Then show how you find information in the text and illustrations.** I found a lot of interesting information, but where can I go to learn more? That's right, I can find information in classroom books or library books, on television programs, from computers, and even from parents and teachers. **Tell children that observation and experimentation are very important in finding out about science and social science too.**

Write *Information Sources* at the top of a piece of chart paper. Have children repeat their suggestions and record them on the chart.

Information Sources

- classroom books
- library books
- TV programs
- computers
- people

Guide practice Now it's your turn. **Give the group science or social science books.** What information can you find in your book from reading? What information can you find in your book from looking at the illustrations? **Have the group tell you what they found.**

On their own Let's all practice finding information. **Have children work with a partner, choosing a book and discussing what information they would like to find in it. Have pairs look through their book, searching for information. As children work, circulate around the room, providing feedback.**

MANAGEMENT TIP

If there is a table of contents or an index in a book, show children how to use it. Model and use corrective feedback as necessary.

Management Lesson 2 Recording Information

Materials chart paper, markers, grade-level science and social science books, writing materials

Introduce Today we're going to practice writing information we've found. Why is it important to keep a record of what we learn? Yes, writing it helps us remember the information and organize it. We can write notes and draw pictures. One way of recording and organizing information is by using a graphic organizer, which is like a picture you write your notes in.

Model **Draw a T-chart on chart paper.** This graphic organizer is called a T-chart. I just read a book about fruit and want to record the information I learned. In the book, I learned about strawberries and apples. **Title the chart** *Fruit.* **Label the first column** *Strawberries* **and the second column** *Apples.* **As you talk about what you read, fill in the appropriate columns.** This graphic organizer shows the information I learned about fruit.

Guide practice Now it's your turn. **Draw another T-chart. Look through a science or social science book with children, finding information. Work with the group to fill in the columns of the chart with the information you found.** What does this graphic organizer show?

On their own Let's all practice recording information in a graphic organizer. **Distribute books to children and have them make their own T-charts to record information from their books. Children may want to use graphic organizers other than T-charts; be sure they are familiar with how the graphic organizer works and if it is an adequate method of recording information. As children work, circulate around the room providing feedback.**

Fruit

Strawberries	Apples
red	red, green, yellow
grow on the ground	grow on trees
seeds outside	seeds inside

MANAGEMENT TIP

Tell children they do not need to write complete sentences in their graphic organizers. Model writing key points and give corrective feedback as necessary.

Management Lesson 3 Communicating Information

Materials grade-level science and social science books

Introduce Today we're going to practice communicating information to other people. What does it mean to communicate? That's right, when we communicate, we share news or information about something. How do we communicate? Yes, we communicate by speaking, by writing, by drawing pictures, and even by using body language. In school, we often communicate information we've found and recorded. We can do that by making a presentation or giving an oral or written report.

Model Listen as I communicate the information I learned in this book. **Model giving a short oral report to the group. The report should be a summary of the contents of a science or social science book, focusing on major points. If you have a poster about the book, use it as a visual support, and point out that using a picture, even one that you have drawn, makes reports clearer and more interesting.**

Guide practice Now it's your turn. **Read to the group a grade-level science or social science book. Then have children communicate information they learned from the book. Have them share only important facts and details. Tell them to speak clearly and at an appropriate volume.**

On their own Let's all practice giving a report. **Divide the class into small groups and give each group several grade-level books related to the weekly concept. Have children choose books and read them (fully or partially), and then communicate information they learned to the rest of their group. You may want to have them draw pictures or create graphic organizers to support their reports. As children work, circulate around the room, modeling as necessary and providing feedback.**

MANAGEMENT 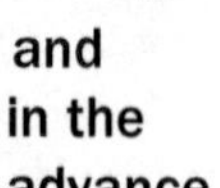

When children find and record information in the future, tell them in advance how they will be asked to communicate that information.

Technology Practice Station

At the Technology Practice Station, both the teacher and children can use computers to access and develop information from software, especially word-processing programs. The teacher and the class can create documents and presentations that will enhance thinking skills and prepare for life-long learning while teaching essential skills. Children can practice keyboarding and other computer skills such as spelling, vocabulary, and language conventions.

Setting Up the Practice Station

Select a place for this station where you have multiple electrical outlets.

- Set up a table with chairs and one or more computers.

Materials

- Scanner

- Video card

- Recording devices

Technology Practice Station

Management Lesson 1   Using Equipment

Materials   computers

· ·

Introduce   Today we're going to talk about using a computer. What do we use computers for? That's right, we use computers for finding information, creating documents, playing games, and sending e-mail. Here we will use computers to create documents and e-mails. Keyboarding is a way to write, and because we are writing, it is important to follow the rules for writing. **Remind children of the rules for writing.** Make sure you understand the activity, think about how to write your own thoughts, work the entire time, and do not disturb others.

Introduce the computer screen, keyboard, mouse, printer, and any other features children may use.

Model   To use a computer, the first thing you have to do is turn it on. **Turn on your computer. When the logon screen appears, use the username and password you want the children to use.** After you turn on the computer, the logon window appears. There are two boxes in it. In the first box, type [children's username]. **Demonstrate how to use the mouse to move the cursor to the second box. In this** box, type [children's password]. Then use the mouse to click OK. **On the board, write the username and password you want the children to use.**

When you're finished using the computer, log off. **Model logging off the computer. Point out that the computer is still on, but can't be used until someone logs on again.**

Guide practice   Call out the parts of the computer, having students point to each as they hear it. Then walk them through logging on and off the computer. Answer questions and model as necessary.

On their own   Let's all practice logging on. Have the children log on and off at individual computers, taking turns if necessary. Circulate around the room, providing feedback. Use the new terms they've learned as you do so.

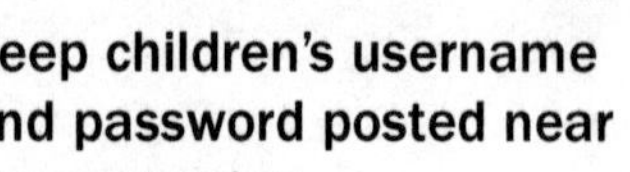

MANAGEMENT

Keep children's username and password posted near the computer.

Technology Practice Station

Management Lesson 2 — Using a Word Processing Program

Materials chart paper, markers, list of spelling words, computers, printer

Introduce Today we're going to practice using a word processing program on our computer. Why might we want to use a computer to create documents? Yes, we use a computer to create documents because we can print out neat, organized papers; we can save our work for another time; and we can practice using the keyboard, a skill we'll always need at school and at home. Today we're going to create a document and print it out.

Model **Before beginning, log on, using children's username and password.**

Here is the icon that opens the word processing program. I'll click it. Here is the icon for opening a document. Now I'll click this. First, I type my name. **Make sure the children know how to use the Shift key to type capital letters.** Now I'll type a list of our spelling words for the week. Here is the printer icon. **Explain where the document will print out. Click the icon, go to the printer, and show them the printed paper.** The words on the screen are now on my paper!

On the chart, write _Creating a Document_. What did I do first? That's right, I opened the word processing program. **What did I do after that?** Right, I typed my name. Then I typed the spelling words. **And last?** Yes, I printed out my document. **Record children's answers on the chart.**

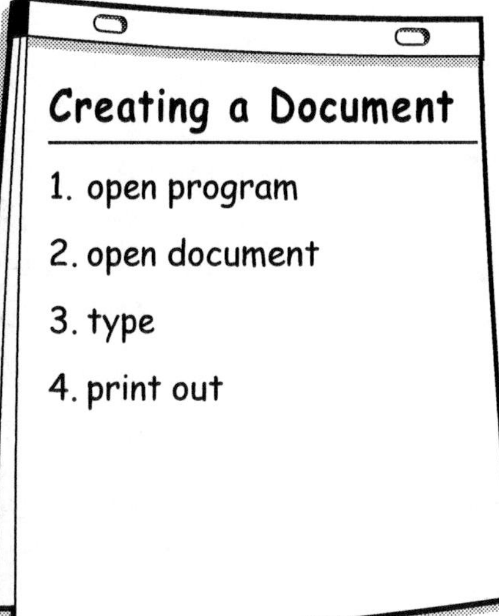

Guide practice Now, it's your turn. **Walk the children through opening the word processing program, having them identify and point to the icons for opening a document and for printing.**

On their own Let's all practice using the word processing program. On your computer, I want you to open a new document, type your name, and print out your page. **As children work, circulate among the group, providing corrective feedback.**

MANAGEMENT 

Keep plenty of computer paper stocked in the printer. If possible, "color code" the activities, using different colors of paper for different activities.

Technology Practice Station

Management Lesson 3 — Sending E-mail

Materials chart paper, markers, computers

Introduce Today we're going to practice sending an e-mail. What is an e-mail? That's right, an e-mail is an electronic letter. You don't need a stamp, and you don't have to wait for the post office to deliver it. How do you send an e-mail? Yes, you use a computer.

Model **If necessary, log on, using the children's username and password.**

Here is the icon that opens the e-mail program. I'll click on it. Here is where I click to start a new message. **Model filling in the To line, making clear that you need to enter a complete e-mail address (name + @ + ISP). Then model filling in the subject line.** Now I'll type a short message, beginning with *Hi, [name]* and ending with *Bye,* and my name. Here is the Send button. I'll click it and wait while my message is sent. It just takes a second.

On the chart, write *Sending E-mail.* **What did I do in order to send an e-mail? Record children's answers in the correct order on the chart. Remind them about using a complete e-mail address and about beginning and closing the message appropriately.**

Guide practice Now it's your turn. **Walk the group through opening the e-mail program and starting a new message.** Now I want each of you to send me an e-mail. **Write your classroom e-mail address on the board and tell children to type it into the To line. Write this on the board:** *Hi from _____.* **Tell the children to use this as their subject line, filling in the blank with their names.**

On their own Have children work independently to write their messages. Before they start, remind them to use *Hi* and *Bye.* Circulate among the group, providing corrective feedback. When they are finished, point out the Send button again, and have them click it.

MANAGEMENT TIP

Have children use proper spelling as they type their e-mails. Model and provide corrective feedback as necessary.

Multi Practice Station

At the Multi Practice Station, children work on a variety of activities in the areas of art, drama, music, math, and health. These activities provide opportunities for children to extend concepts learned during the week by combining literacy with the arts, math, and health.

Setting Up the Practice Station

Provide a table or arrange a group of desks where children can create art projects.

- Gather art materials such as paper, markers, crayons, rulers, and any other items that are specific to the week's activity.

- Store materials in a plastic bin for easier clean up and storage.

- Restock items as necessary.

Student Routine

- **Art** Create a simple portfolio for storage of artwork samples. Staple two pieces of poster board together and decorate. Add samples of your artwork each week.

- **Drama** *Improvisation* is performing without a script and without preparation. Perform a dialogue between two of the characters from this week's selection, or discuss the topic or theme for three minutes.

- **Music** Keep a music journal listing the types of music you've heard at the station. List the title and artist of each piece and explain why you liked or didn't like the piece, as well as any other thoughts.

- **Math** Read through the entire problem, and then write the pieces of information given. Use what you know to help solve the problem.

- **Health** After completing each Health Station activity, write a health tip in your journal.

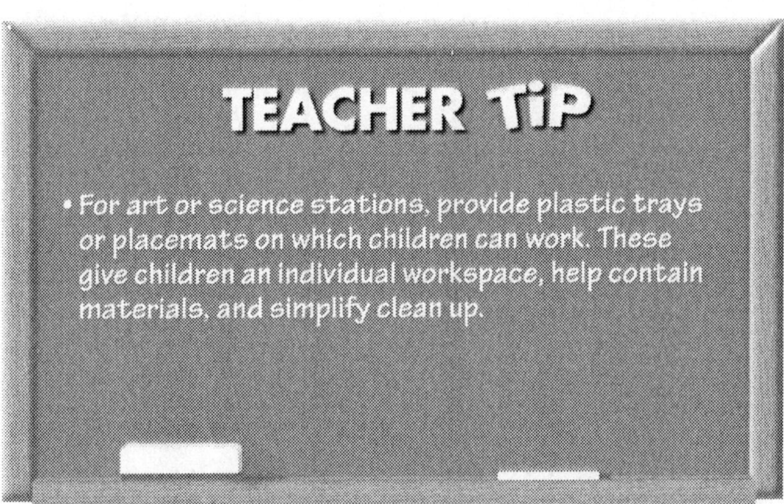

Assessing Station Activities

Using Assessment to Guide Instruction Informal, ongoing assessments are an important means of guiding classroom instruction, and station activities provide excellent opportunities for ongoing assessments.

Practice Station time is an extension of your lesson. It provides an opportunity for you to work with small groups, but it is not "busy time" for the other children. Practice Station time provides a wonderful opportunity for you to assess how well children can apply what you have taught. The work they do during Practice Station time is an important piece of your assessment of the whole child!

There are many formal and informal ways to assess children and their work. Many of these assessments include children assessing their own work. Use the activities throughout the school year to measure children's growth and development.

The following assessment tools may be helpful as you informally assess children's Practice Station work.

Rubrics

- Create simple pictorial rubrics to guide children in assessing their own work.

- Use a rubric to guide your assessment of children's creativity and motivation.

Portfolios

- Save work children complete during Practice Station time. Use portfolio contents to measure children's progress and growth over time.

Informal Observations

- You may want to use a notebook or the Observation Record on p. 31 to record your observations of children.

- Divide the class into small groups. Focus on observing a small group of children during Practice Station time each day instead of trying to observe all children's behaviors.

- Determine ahead of time what you will observe each week. Perhaps it is social interactions or emotional development. Some weeks you may wish to focus on academic development. Determining your expectations will help narrow your assessment.

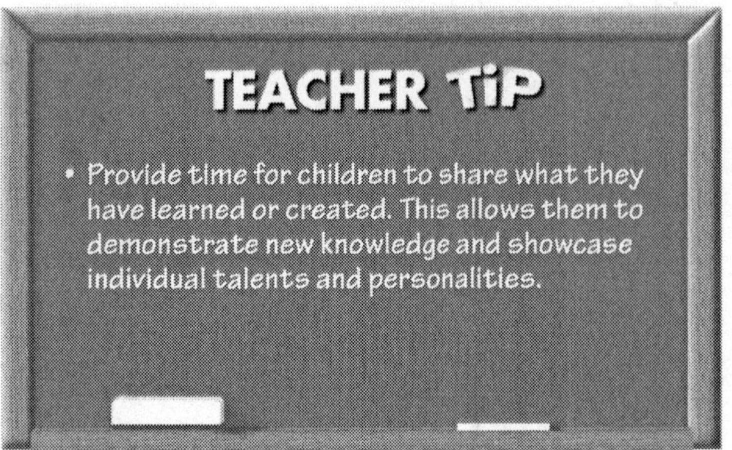

Observation Record

Date .... Child...

Date .... Child...

Date .... Child...

Date .... Child...

Date .... Child...

Date .... Child...

Student Work Plans

What Are Student Work Plans?

Pages 33–68 contain lesson-specific reproducible work plans for children to use during their independent activity time. Each work plan lists the tasks that children will complete, in Practice Stations or independently, while you meet with small groups. The work plans help children remember their assignments, plan their time, and keep track of what they've done. Work plans allow children to take responsibility and will aid them in becoming successful independent learners.

How Do I Use the Student Work Plans?

Begin by explaining the activities in the Practice Stations to children. Then distribute copies of *My Work Plan* and review the tasks. Be sure children understand that they will check the box next to each task as they complete it. Remind children that if they finish an activity before time is up, they can answer the Wrap Up Your Week questions, complete the Early Finishers activity, or visit the classroom library. At the end of the week, you can collect children's work plans, or you can send them home.

If you prefer, you can customize a work plan for one or more children or for use during a particular lesson. For this purpose, a generic work plan can be found on p. 69.

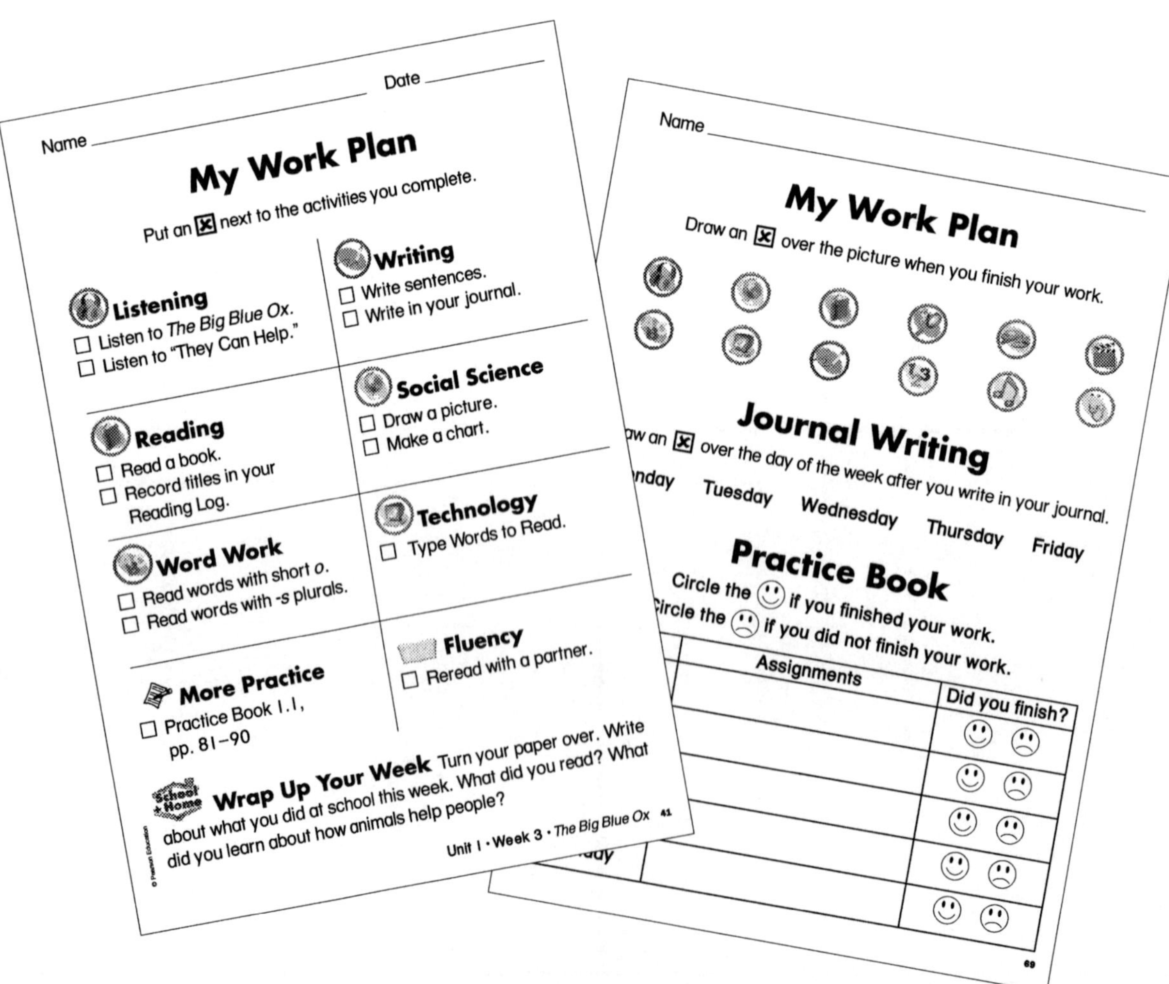

My Work Plan

Put an ☒ next to the activities you complete.

Listening

- ☐ Listen to *Sam.*
- ☐ Listen to "Where Do You Sleep?"

Writing

- ☐ Complete a sentence using a noun.
- ☐ Write in your journal.

Reading

- ☐ Read a book.
- ☐ Record titles in your Reading Log.

Science

- ☐ Describe where objects are.
- ☐ Classify objects.

Word Work

- ☐ Read words with initial consonant *s* and consonant *t.*

Technology

- ☐ Type words.
- ☐ Print your words.

More Practice

- ☐ Practice Book 1.1, pp. 1–10

Fluency

- ☐ Reread with a partner.

School + Home **Wrap Up Your Week** Turn your paper over. Write about what you did at school this week. What did you read? What did you learn about the things around you?

My Work Plan

Put an ☒ next to the activities you complete.

Listening
☐ Listen to *Snap!*
☐ Listen to "Families."

Writing
☐ Write a title and list.
☐ Write in your journal.

Reading
☐ Read a book.
☐ Record titles in your Reading Log.

Social Science
☐ Think about being your best.
☐ Make a picture with a title.

Word Work
☐ Read words with initial consonant sound /k/ spelled *c*.

Technology
☐ Type words.
☐ Print your words.

More Practice
☐ Practice Book 1.1, pp. 11–20

Fluency
☐ Reread with a partner.

School + Home **Wrap Up Your Week** Turn your paper over. Write about what you did at school this week. What did you read? What did you learn about homes and families?

My Work Plan

Put an ⊠ next to the activities you complete.

 ## Listening

- ☐ Listen to *Where Is Tip?*
- ☐ Listen to "Yards."

 ## Writing

- ☐ Write a title and a list.
- ☐ Write in your journal.

Reading

- ☐ Read a book.
- ☐ Record titles in your Reading Log.

 ## Science

- ☐ Name parts of a tree.
- ☐ Make a poster.

 ## Word Work

- ☐ Read words with initial and final consonants *b* and *g.*

 ## Technology

- ☐ Type words.
- ☐ Print your words.

 ## More Practice

- ☐ Practice Book 1.1, pp. 21–30

 ## Fluency

- ☐ Reread with a partner.

Wrap Up Your Week Turn your paper over. Write about what you did at school this week. What did you read? What did you learn about families?

My Work Plan

Put an ☒ next to the activities you complete.

🎧 Listening

☐ Listen to *A Big Mess.*
☐ Listen to "Around the Block."

✏️ Writing

☐ Write a verb to complete a sentence.
☐ Write in your journal.

📖 Reading

☐ Read a book.
☐ Record titles in your Reading Log.

🌐 Social Science

☐ Draw shapes.
☐ Make a map.

🔤 Word Work

☐ Read words with final consonants *d, g, ll, m, p,* and *t.*

💻 Technology

☐ Type words.
☐ Print your words.

📝 More Practice

☐ Practice Book 1.1, pp. 31–40

📘 Fluency

☐ Reread with a partner.

School + Home **Wrap Up Your Week** Turn your paper over. Write about what you did at school this week. What did you read? What did you learn about neighborhoods?

My Work Plan

Put an **☒** next to the activities you complete.

Listening

- ☐ Listen to *School Day.*
- ☐ Listen to "How Do You Get to School?"

Writing

- ☐ Write a verb to complete a sentence.
- ☐ Write in your journal.

Reading

- ☐ Read a book.
- ☐ Record titles in your Reading Log.

Social Science

- ☐ Follow rules.
- ☐ Make a list of rules.

Word Work

- ☐ Read words with initial consonant *j* and consonant *k.*

Technology

- ☐ Type words.
- ☐ Print your words.

More Practice

- ☐ Practice Book 1.1, pp. 41–50

Fluency

- ☐ Reread with a partner.

School + Home

Wrap Up Your Week Turn your paper over. Write about what you did at school this week. What did you read? What did you learn about getting to school?

My Work Plan

Put an **☒** next to the activities you complete.

Listening

- ☐ Listen to *Farmers Market.*
- ☐ Listen to "Our Food."

Writing

- ☐ Write a noun and a descriptive word to complete a sentence.
- ☐ Write in your journal.

Reading

- ☐ Read a book.
- ☐ Record titles in your Reading Log.

Science

- ☐ Classify food.
- ☐ Make a poster.

Word Work

- ☐ Read words with *V, v* and *Z, z.*

Technology

- ☐ Type words.
- ☐ Print your words.

More Practice

- ☐ Practice Book 1.1, pp. 51–60

Fluency

- ☐ Reread with a partner.

School + Home **Wrap Up Your Week** Turn your paper over. Write about what you did at school this week. What did you read? What did you learn about buying food in the neighborhood?

My Work Plan

Put an **☒** next to the activities you complete.

Listening

- ☐ Listen to *Sam, Come Back!*
- ☐ Listen to "Puppy Games."

Writing

- ☐ Write a list.
- ☐ Write in your journal.

Reading

- ☐ Read a book.
- ☐ Record titles in your Reading Log.

Science

- ☐ Write about a pet's needs.
- ☐ Make a class book.

Word Work

- ☐ Read words with short *a*.
- ☐ Read words with final *ck*.

Technology

- ☐ Type short *a* words.

More Practice

- ☐ Practice Book 1.1, pp. 61–70

Fluency

- ☐ Reread with a partner.

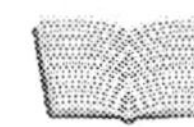
Wrap Up Your Week Turn your paper over. Write about what you did at school this week. What did you read? What did you learn about what pets need?

My Work Plan

Put an ☒ next to the activities you complete.

Listening
- ☐ Listen to *Pig in a Wig.*
- ☐ Listen to "We Are Vets."

Writing
- ☐ Write sentences.
- ☐ Write in your journal.

Reading
- ☐ Read a book.
- ☐ Record titles in your Reading Log.

Social Science
- ☐ Draw a picture.
- ☐ Write the job name.

Word Work
- ☐ Read words with short *i.*
- ☐ Read words with final *x.*

Technology
- ☐ Type Words to Read.

More Practice
- ☐ Practice Book 1.1, pp. 71–80

Fluency
- ☐ Reread with a partner.

School + Home **Wrap Up Your Week** Turn your paper over. Write about what you did at school this week. What did you read? What did you learn about people who help animals?

My Work Plan

Put an ☒ next to the activities you complete.

 **Listening**

- ☐ Listen to *The Big Blue Ox.*
- ☐ Listen to "They Can Help."

 **Writing**

- ☐ Write sentences.
- ☐ Write in your journal.

 **Reading**

- ☐ Read a book.
- ☐ Record titles in your Reading Log.

Social Science

- ☐ Draw a picture.
- ☐ Make a chart.

 **Word Work**

- ☐ Read words with short *o.*
- ☐ Read words with *-s* plurals.

 **Technology**

- ☐ Type Words to Read.

 **More Practice**

- ☐ Practice Book 1.1, pp. 81–90

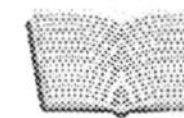 **Fluency**

- ☐ Reread with a partner.

School + Home **Wrap Up Your Week** Turn your paper over. Write about what you did at school this week. What did you read? What did you learn about how animals help people?

My Work Plan

Put an ☒ next to the activities you complete.

Listening

- ☐ Listen to *Whales.*
- ☐ Listen to "Oh, Brave Bald Eagle, Soar."

Writing

- ☐ Write sentences.
- ☐ Write in your journal.

Reading

- ☐ Read a book.
- ☐ Record titles in your Reading Log.

Science

- ☐ Make a poster.
- ☐ Color pictures.

Word Work

- ☐ Read words ending with *-s.*
- ☐ Read words ending with *-ing.*

Technology

- ☐ Type Words to Read.

More Practice

- ☐ Practice Book 1.1, pp. 91–100

Fluency

- ☐ Reread with a partner.

School + Home Wrap Up Your Week Turn your paper over. Write about what you did at school this week. What did you read? What did you learn about helping wild animals?

My Work Plan

Put an ☒ next to the activities you complete.

Listening

☐ Listen to *Get the Egg!*
☐ Listen to "Help the Birds."

Writing

☐ Write statements.
☐ Write in your journal.

Reading

☐ Read a book.
☐ Record titles in your
  Reading Log.

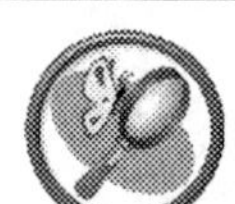

Science

☐ Draw an animal.
☐ Label it.

Word Work

☐ Read words with short *e.*
☐ Read words with blends.

Technology

☐ Type a list of short *e* words.

More Practice

☐ Practice Book 1.1,
  pp. 101–110

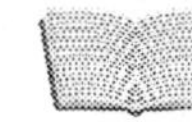

Fluency

☐ Reread with a partner.

School + Home **Wrap Up Your Week** Turn your paper over. Write about what you did at school this week. What did you read? What did you learn about wild animals in your neighborhood?

My Work Plan

Put an ☒ next to the activities you complete.

Listening

- ☐ Listen to *Animal Park.*
- ☐ Listen to poetry.

Writing

- ☐ Write questions.
- ☐ Write in your journal.

Reading

- ☐ Read a book.
- ☐ Record titles in your Reading Log.

Science

- ☐ Make a diorama.
- ☐ Present the diorama.

Word Work

- ☐ Read words with short *u.*
- ☐ Read words with blends.

Technology

- ☐ Type a list of short *u* words.

More Practice

- ☐ Practice Book 1.1, pp. 111–120

Fluency

- ☐ Reread with a partner.

School + Home **Wrap Up Your Week** Turn your paper over. Write about what you did at school this week. What did you read? What did you learn about watching wild animals?

My Work Plan

Put an ☒ next to the activities you complete.

Listening
- ☐ Listen to *A Big Fish for Max.*
- ☐ Listen to "At Home."

Writing
- ☐ Make a list of nouns.
- ☐ Write in your journal.

Reading
- ☐ Read a book.
- ☐ Record titles in your Reading Log.

Social Science
- ☐ Make a T-chart.
- ☐ Label pictures.

Word Work
- ☐ Read words with *sh, th.*
- ☐ Read words with sounds of *a.*

Technology
- ☐ Type a list of spelling words.

More Practice
- ☐ Practice Book 1.1, pp. 121–130

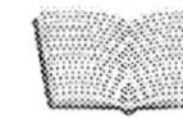

Fluency
- ☐ Reread with a partner.

School + Home **Wrap Up Your Week** Turn your paper over. Write about what you did at school this week. What did you read? What did you learn about families working and playing together?

My Work Plan

Put an ☒ next to the activities you complete.

Listening
- ☐ Listen to *The Farmer in the Hat.*
- ☐ Listen to "Helping Hands at 4-H."

Reading
- ☐ Read a book.
- ☐ Record titles in your Reading Log.

Word Work
- ☐ Read words with long *a*.
- ☐ Read words with *c* and *g*.

More Practice
- ☐ Practice Book 1.1, pp. 131–140

Writing
- ☐ Write sentences with proper nouns.
- ☐ Write in your journal.

Social Science
- ☐ Make a poster.

Technology
- ☐ Type long *a* words.

Fluency
- ☐ Reread with a partner.

School + Home **Wrap Up Your Week** Turn your paper over. Write about what you did at school this week. What did you read? What did you learn about school as a community?

My Work Plan

Put an ☒ next to the activities you complete.

 **Listening**

☐ Listen to *Who Works Here?*
☐ Listen to "Neighborhood Map."

 **Writing**

☐ Write sentences about helpers.
☐ Write in your journal.

 **Reading**

☐ Read a book.
☐ Record titles in your Reading Log.

Social Science

☐ Draw a building.

 **Word Work**

☐ Read words with long *i*.
☐ Read words with *wh, ch, tch*.

 **Technology**

☐ Type special titles.

 **More Practice**

☐ Practice Book 1.1, pp. 141–150

 **Fluency**

☐ Reread with a partner.

School + Home **Wrap Up Your Week** Turn your paper over. Write about what you did at school this week. What did you read? What did you learn about people who make your community a nice place?

My Work Plan

Put an **X** next to the activities you complete.

🎧 Listening

- ☐ Listen to *The Big Circle.*
- ☐ Listen to "We Are Safe Together."

✏️ Writing

- ☐ Write sentences.
- ☐ Write in your journal.

📖 Reading

- ☐ Read a book.
- ☐ Record titles in your Reading Log.

🔬 Science

- ☐ Draw a picture.
- ☐ Make a T-chart.

🔤 Word Work

- ☐ Read words with long *o.*
- ☐ Read words with contractions.

💻 Technology

- ☐ Type a sentence.

✍️ More Practice

- ☐ Practice Book 1.1, pp. 151–160

📖 Fluency

- ☐ Reread with a partner.

School + Home **Wrap Up Your Week** Turn your paper over. Write about what you did at school this week. What did you read? What did you learn about animal communities working together to survive?

My Work Plan

Put an **☒** next to the activities you complete.

Listening

☐ Listen to *Life in the Forest.*
☐ Listen to "A Mangrove Forest."

Writing

☐ Write using voice.
☐ Write in your journal.

Reading

☐ Read a book.
☐ Record titles in your Reading Log.

Science

☐ Draw a plant or animal.
☐ List information.

Word Work

☐ Read words with long *u* and *e.*
☐ Read words ending with *-ed.*

Technology

☐ Type a sentence with long *u* words.

 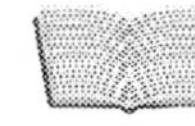

More Practice

☐ Practice Book 1.1, pp. 161–170

Fluency

☐ Reread with a partner.

Wrap Up Your Week Turn your paper over. Write about what you did at school this week. What did you read? What did you learn about plant and animal communities?

My Work Plan

Put an ☒ next to the activities you complete.

Listening

- ☐ Listen to *Honey Bees.*
- ☐ Listen to poetry.

Writing

- ☐ Write sentences with story words.
- ☐ Write in your journal.

Reading

- ☐ Read a book.
- ☐ Record titles in your Reading Log.

Science

- ☐ Sort picture cards.

Word Work

- ☐ Read words with long *e.*
- ☐ Read words with syllables.

Technology

- ☐ Type a sentence with story words.

More Practice

- ☐ Practice Book 1.1, pp. 171–181

Fluency

- ☐ Reread with a partner.

School + Home

Wrap Up Your Week Turn your paper over. Write about what you did at school this week. What did you read? What did you learn about communities of insects and communities of people?

My Work Plan

Put an ⊠ next to the activities you complete.

Listening

- ☐ Listen to *A Place to Play.*
- ☐ Listen to "From Start to Finish."

Writing

- ☐ Write using action verbs.
- ☐ Write in your journal.

Reading

- ☐ Read a book.
- ☐ Record titles in your Reading Log.

Social Science

- ☐ Draw pictures that compare.

Word Work

- ☐ Read words with *y.*
- ☐ Read words with long vowels.

Technology

- ☐ Type a list of spelling words.

More Practice

- ☐ Practice Book 1.2, pp. 1–10

Fluency

- ☐ Reread with a partner.

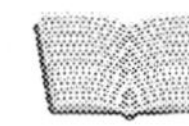

School + Home Wrap Up Your Week Turn your paper over. Write about what you did at school this week. What did you read? What did you learn about how places change?

My Work Plan

Put an ☒ next to the activities you complete.

Listening

- ☐ Listen to *Ruby in Her Own Time.*
- ☐ Listen to "Willy Skates!"

Writing

- ☐ Write sentences in order.
- ☐ Write in your journal.

Reading

- ☐ Read a book.
- ☐ Record titles in your Reading Log.

Social Science

- ☐ Write about yourself.
- ☐ Share your sentences.

Word Work

- ☐ Read words with *ng, nk.*
- ☐ Read compound words.

Technology

- ☐ Type Words to Read.

More Practice

- ☐ Practice Book 1.2, pp. 11–20

Fluency

- ☐ Reread with a partner.

School + Home

Wrap Up Your Week Turn your paper over. Write about what you did at school this week. What did you read? What did you learn about growing and changing?

My Work Plan

Put an ☒ next to the activities you complete.

 **Listening**

☐ Listen to *Jan's New Home.*
☐ Listen to "A Letter from Jan."

 **Writing**

☐ Write using voice.
☐ Write in your journal.

 **Reading**

☐ Read a book.
☐ Record titles in your Reading Log.

 **Social Science**

☐ Find a picture.
☐ List reasons.

 **Word Work**

☐ Read words with *-es.*
☐ Read words with *or* and *ore.*

 **Technology**

☐ Type words with *-es.*

More Practice

☐ Practice Book 1.2, pp. 21–30

 **Fluency**

☐ Reread with a partner.

Wrap Up Your Week Turn your paper over. Write about what you did at school this week. What did you read? What did you learn about exciting changes?

My Work Plan

Put an ☒ next to the activities you complete.

🎧 Listening

☐ Listen to *A Storm Comes.*
☐ Listen to "Weather Tools."

✏️ Writing

☐ Write sentences.
☐ Write in your journal.

📖 Reading

☐ Read a book.
☐ Record titles in your Reading Log.

🔍 Science

☐ Make a T-chart.
☐ Write two lists.

🔤 Word Work

☐ Read words ending with *-ed* and *-ing.*
☐ Read words with *ar.*

💻 Technology

☐ Type sentences with story words.

📝 More Practice

☐ Practice Book 1.2, pp. 31–40

📖 Fluency

☐ Reread with a partner.

Wrap Up Your Week Turn your paper over. Write about what you did at school this week. What did you read? What did you learn about how weather changes?

My Work Plan

Put an **☒** next to the activities you complete.

Listening

☐ Listen to *Fall Is Here.*
☐ Listen to "My Computer."

Writing

☐ Write about fall.
☐ Write in your journal.

Reading

☐ Read a book.
☐ Record titles in your Reading Log.

Science

☐ Rub leaves.
☐ Write descriptions.

Word Work

☐ Read words with *er, ir, ur.*
☐ Read words with contractions.

Technology

☐ Type words with *er, ir, ur.*

More Practice

☐ Practice Book 1.2, pp. 41–50

Fluency

☐ Reread with a partner.

Wrap Up Your Week Turn your paper over. Write about what you did at school this week. What did you read? What did you learn about changes throughout the seasons?

My Work Plan

Put an ☒ next to the activities you complete.

🎧 Listening

☐ Listen to *Where Are My Animal Friends?*
☐ Listen to poetry.

📖 Reading

☐ Read a book.
☐ Record titles in your Reading Log.

Word Work

☐ Read words with *-er, -est.*
☐ Read words with *dge.*

✏️ Writing

☐ Write sentences with contractions.
☐ Write in your journal.

🔍 Science

☐ Make a graph.
☐ Write about weather.

💻 Technology

☐ Type a list of words with *-er* and *-est.*

More Practice

☐ Practice Book 1.2, pp. 51–60

Fluency

☐ Reread with a partner.

School + Home **Wrap Up Your Week** Turn your paper over. Write about what you did at school this week. What did you read? What did you learn about what animals do when the seasons change?

My Work Plan

Put an ⊠ next to the activities you complete.

Listening

☐ Listen to *Mama's Birthday Present.*
☐ Listen to "Chinese Surprises."

Writing

☐ Write an invitation.
☐ Write in your journal.

Reading

☐ Read a book.
☐ Record titles in your Reading Log.

Social Science

☐ Plan a party.
☐ Make a list.

Word Work

☐ Read words with *ai, ay.*
☐ Read possessive words.

Technology

☐ Type sentences with adjectives.

More Practice

☐ Practice Book 1.2, pp. 61–70

Fluency

☐ Reread with a partner.

Wrap Up Your Week Turn your paper over. Write about what you did at school this week. What did you read? What did you learn about surprises and treasures?

My Work Plan

Put an ☒ next to the activities you complete.

Listening

- ☐ Listen to *The Dot.*
- ☐ Listen to "Meet José Ramirez."

Writing

- ☐ Write a list of adjectives.
- ☐ Write in your journal.

Reading

- ☐ Read a book.
- ☐ Record titles in your Reading Log.

Social Science

- ☐ Study a painting.
- ☐ Write notes.

Word Work

- ☐ Read words with *ea.*
- ☐ Read words with endings.

Technology

- ☐ Type a list of spelling words.

More Practice

- ☐ Practice Book 1.2, pp. 71–80

Fluency

- ☐ Reread with a partner.

School + Home **Wrap Up Your Week** Turn your paper over. Write about what you did at school this week. What did you read? What did you learn about treasures you can create?

My Work Plan

Put an ☒ next to the activities you complete.

🎧 Listening

- ☐ Listen to *A Trip to Washington, D.C.*
- ☐ Listen to "Famous Places in America."

✍ Writing

- ☐ Write a description.
- ☐ Write in your journal.

📖 Reading

- ☐ Read a book.
- ☐ Record titles in your Reading Log.

🌐 Social Science

- ☐ Make a T-chart.
- ☐ Write two lists.

Word Work

- ☐ Read words with *oa, ow*.
- ☐ Read words with blends.

💻 Technology

- ☐ Type sentences with story words.

More Practice

- ☐ Practice Book 1.2, pp. 81–90

Fluency

- ☐ Reread with a partner.

School + Home **Wrap Up Your Week** Turn your paper over. Write about what you did at school this week. What did you read? What did you learn about treasures in your country?

My Work Plan

Put an ☒ next to the activities you complete.

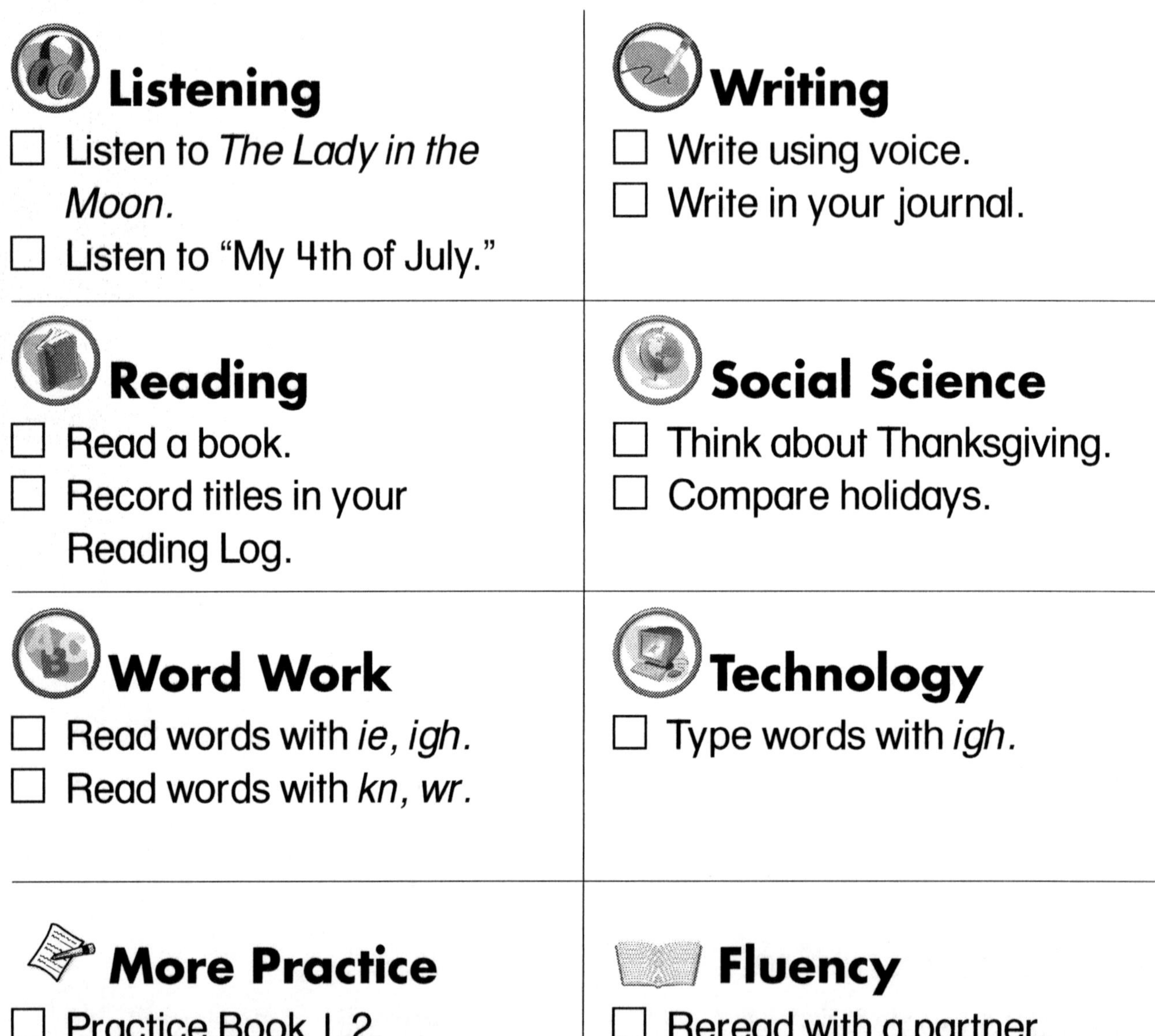

Listening
- ☐ Listen to *The Lady in the Moon.*
- ☐ Listen to "My 4th of July."

Writing
- ☐ Write using voice.
- ☐ Write in your journal.

Reading
- ☐ Read a book.
- ☐ Record titles in your Reading Log.

Social Science
- ☐ Think about Thanksgiving.
- ☐ Compare holidays.

Word Work
- ☐ Read words with *ie, igh.*
- ☐ Read words with *kn, wr.*

Technology
- ☐ Type words with *igh.*

More Practice
- ☐ Practice Book 1.2, pp. 91–100

Fluency
- ☐ Reread with a partner.

School + Home **Wrap Up Your Week** Turn your paper over. Write about what you did at school this week. What did you read? What did you learn about treasuring special days?

My Work Plan

Put an ☒ next to the activities you complete.

Listening

- ☐ Listen to *Peter's Chair*.
- ☐ Listen to "Peter's Baby Sister."

Writing

- ☐ Write sentences.
- ☐ Write in your journal.

Reading

- ☐ Read a book.
- ☐ Record titles in your Reading Log.

Social Science

- ☐ Draw pictures.
- ☐ Write about each picture.

Word Work

- ☐ Read compound words.
- ☐ Read words with *ew, ue, ui.*

Technology

- ☐ Type and underline compound words.

More Practice

- ☐ Practice Book 1.2, pp. 101–110

Fluency

- ☐ Reread with a partner.

School + Home

Wrap Up Your Week Turn your paper over. Write about what you did at school this week. What did you read? What did you learn about treasures you can share?

My Work Plan

Put an ☒ next to the activities you complete.

🎧 Listening

- ☐ Listen to *Henry and Mudge and Mrs. Hopper's House.*
- ☐ Listen to poetry.

✍ Writing

- ☐ Write using vivid adjectives.
- ☐ Write in your journal.

📖 Reading

- ☐ Read a book.
- ☐ Record titles in your Reading Log.

🌐 Social Science

- ☐ Color and label things you treasure.
- ☐ Share with a partner.

Word Work

- ☐ Read words with suffixes.
- ☐ Read words with *oo.*

💻 Technology

- ☐ Type a list of Words to Read.

More Practice

- ☐ Practice Book 1.2, pp. 111–120

Fluency

- ☐ Reread with a partner.

School + Home **Wrap Up Your Week** Turn your paper over. Write about what you did at school this week. What did you read? What did you learn about treasures we share with neighbors?

My Work Plan

Put an ☒ next to the activities you complete.

 ## Listening

☐ Listen to *Tippy-Toe Chick, Go!*
☐ Listen to "Little Red Hen."

 ## Writing

☐ Write commands.
☐ Write in your journal.

 ## Reading

☐ Read a book.
☐ Record titles in your Reading Log.

 ## Science

☐ Play a matching game.

 ## Word Work

☐ Read words with *ow.*
☐ Read words ending with *le.*

 ## Technology

☐ Write an e-mail.

More Practice

☐ Practice Book 1.2, pp. 121–130

Fluency

☐ Reread with a partner.

School + Home **Wrap Up Your Week** Turn your paper over. Write about what you did at school this week. What did you read? What did you learn about solving problems?

My Work Plan

Put an ☒ next to the activities you complete.

Listening

- ☐ Listen to *Mole and the Baby Bird.*
- ☐ Listen to "Dear Dr. Know-It-All."

Writing

- ☐ Write a journal entry.

Reading

- ☐ Read a book.
- ☐ Record titles in your Reading Log.

Social Science

- ☐ Write about citizenship.
- ☐ Draw a picture.

Word Work

- ☐ Read words with *ou.*
- ☐ Read words and syllables.

Technology

- ☐ Type exclamations.

More Practice

- ☐ Practice Book 1.2, pp. 131–140

Fluency

- ☐ Reread with a partner.

School + Home **Wrap Up Your Week** Turn your paper over. Write about what you did at school this week. What did you read? What did you learn about looking at things in a different way?

My Work Plan

Put an ☒ next to the activities you complete.

Listening

- ☐ Listen to *Dot & Jabber*.
- ☐ Listen to "Water."

Writing

- ☐ Write sentences and proofread.
- ☐ Write in your journal.

Reading

- ☐ Read a book.
- ☐ Record titles in your Reading Log.

Science

- ☐ Draw a tree.
- ☐ Label its parts.

Word Work

- ☐ Read words with *oo.*
- ☐ Read words with endings.

Technology

- ☐ Type different kinds of sentences.

More Practice

- ☐ Practice Book 1.2, pp. 141–150

Fluency

- ☐ Reread with a partner.

School + Home

Wrap Up Your Week Turn your paper over. Write about what you did at school this week. What did you read? What did you learn about solving mysteries?

My Work Plan

Put an ☒ next to the activities you complete.

🎧 Listening
- ☐ Listen to *Boat Travelers*.
- ☐ Listen to "Roy's Wheelchair."

✍️ Writing
- ☐ Write sentences with pronouns.
- ☐ Write in your journal.

📖 Reading
- ☐ Read a book.
- ☐ Record titles in your Reading Log.

🌎 Social Science
- ☐ Draw two boats.
- ☐ Write about how they are different.

🔤 Word Work
- ☐ Read words with *oi, oy*.
- ☐ Read words with suffixes.

💻 Technology
- ☐ Write an e-mail.

📝 More Practice
- ☐ Practice Book 1.2, pp. 151–160

📖 Fluency
- ☐ Reread with a partner.

School + Home **Wrap Up Your Week** Turn your paper over. Write about what you did at school this week. What did you read? What did you learn about ideas that make our lives easier?

My Work Plan

Put an ☒ next to the activities you complete.

Listening
- ☐ Listen to *Alexander Graham Bell.*
- ☐ Listen to "Inventions."

Writing
- ☐ Write sentences using *I.*
- ☐ Write in your journal.

Reading
- ☐ Read a book.
- ☐ Record titles in your Reading Log.

Social Science
- ☐ Choose an invention.
- ☐ Fill in sentences.

Word Work
- ☐ Read words with *aw, au.*
- ☐ Read words with short *e.*

Technology
- ☐ Type sentences with story words.

More Practice
- ☐ Practice Book 1.2, pp. 161–170

Fluency
- ☐ Reread with a partner.

Wrap Up Your Week Turn your paper over. Write about what you did at school this week. What did you read? What did you learn about how great ideas change the way we live?

My Work Plan

Put an ⊠ next to the activities you complete.

🎧 Listening

☐ Listen to *The Stone Garden.*
☐ Listen to poetry.

✏️ Writing

☐ Write different kinds of sentences.
☐ Write in your journal.

📖 Reading

☐ Read a book.
☐ Record titles in your Reading Log.

Social Science

☐ Make a plan.
☐ List people who can help you.

Word Work

☐ Read words with prefixes.
☐ Read words with long vowels.

Technology

☐ Type a list of pronouns.

More Practice

☐ Practice Book 1.2, pp. 171–180

Fluency

☐ Reread with a partner.

School + Home

Wrap Up Your Week Turn your paper over. Write about what you did at school this week. What did you read? What did you learn about what happens with a new idea?

My Work Plan

Draw an ⊠ over the picture when you finish your work.

Journal Writing

Draw an ⊠ over the day of the week after you write in your journal.

Monday   Tuesday   Wednesday   Thursday   Friday

Practice Book

Circle the ☺ if you finished your work.

Circle the ☹ if you did not finish your work.

	Assignments	Did you finish?
Monday		☺ ☹
Tuesday		☺ ☹
Wednesday		☺ ☹
Thursday		☺ ☹
Friday		☺ ☹

Name ______________________________

My Reading Log

Date	What is the title?	Who is the author?	What did you think of it?